Pimp Your Pumps

35 easy ways to transform your shoes

Charlotte Liddle

CICO **kidz**

I would like to dedicate this book to my little boy, Syd. I hope that one day we can make dinosaur slippers together, and you too can share in my love for crafts.

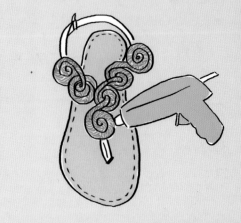

Published in 2014 by CICO Kidz
An imprint of Ryland Peters & Small Ltd

20–21 Jockey's Fields   519 Broadway, 5th Floor
London WC1R 4BW   New York, NY 10012

www.rylandpeters.com

10 9 8 7 6 5 4 3 2 1

Text © Charlotte Liddle 2014
Design and photography © CICO Kidz 2014

A CIP catalog record for this book is available from the Library of Congress and the British Library.

ISBN: 978 1 78249 106 4

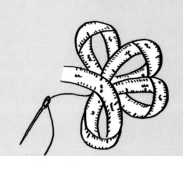

Editor: Marie Clayton
Designer: Geoff Borin
Photographers: Terry Benson, Jo Henderson
Stylists: Rob Merrett, Sophie Martell

For digital editions, visit www.cicobooks.com/apps.php

Printed in China

Contents

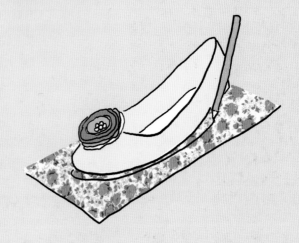

Introduction

While still at college I was lucky enough to sell my first design—a pair of embellished ballet pumps. So you can imagine how excited I was when I was asked to create a book about upcycling and customizing shoes!

This book features lots of traditional craft techniques—such as hand and machine sewing, ribbon embroidery, and weaving—as well as more innovative ideas, such as making charms from shrink plastic. It teaches how to use fabric and spray paints, stencils, dyes, and pens to change the look or color of your shoes. If you love a hint of sparkle there are lots of cool ideas for making 3-D embellishments as well as adding beads, buttons, rhinestones, and even old pieces of jewelry to bring a bit of bling. All of the projects have step-by-step instructions with illustrations and have been given a skill level rating to make it easy for you to identify the ones you would like to try. There is a handy techniques section and lots of advice on how and where to buy inexpensive shoes to decorate and how to look after and clean your old shoes ready for upcycling—as well as plenty of "making" hints and tips throughout.

The book is split into five chapters. Flowers and Fancies features lots of my top embellishment techniques, such as zipper flowers, ribbon roses, and fabric yoyos. Sequins and Sparkle is jam-packed with a whole array of ways to add a bit of glitz to your sneakers and ballet pumps, while Animal Magic shows you how to make animal and dinosaur slippers and cute cat and mouse pumps. Fabric and Ribbons is a great chapter to develop your sewing skills and the Paper, Paint, and Plastic chapter shows you how to use all those different materials to make galaxy-effect canvas sneakers, funky collaged shoes, and lots more!

I really hope you have some fun with this book; why not have a pimp your pumps party? Get everyone to collect old fabrics, paints, and bits of broken jewelry and you will have endless fun re-inventing tired or boring shoes, pumps, sneakers, and rain boots!

Skill levels

✿ Easy first projects that can be done without adult help

✿✿ Still fairly easy, but you may need adult help with some steps

✿✿✿ These will take a bit more time, use slightly more complicated techniques, or will need adult help

Techniques

Embroidery and stitching

Some of the projects use simple stitching techniques and this section shows you how to work them.

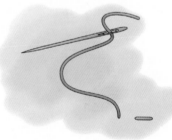

Securing the thread end

At the start of your stitching, and when you have finished sewing, secure the thread end by sewing a few tiny stitches over and over in the same place on the back of the fabric. Then trim off the thread end.

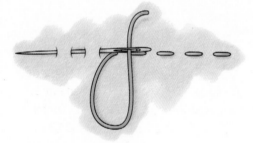

Running or gathering stitch

A long, straight stitch made by hand, used as a decorative stitch or to gather fabric. For gathering, the stitches should be fairly loose so they can be drawn up to gather the fabric evenly.

Back stitch

Back stitch is a very useful stitch because it gives the effect of a continuous line.

1 Bring the thread up through the fabric then work a stitch backward. Go down through the fabric and underneath, and come up a stitch length in front of the last stitch.

2 Work the next stitch backward to meet the end of the first stitch worked, again coming up a stitch length in front. Repeat to make a continuous line of stitching.

Blanket stitch

1 Bring the thread out through the fabric at the top of the stitch. Take a vertical stitch through the fabric a short distance away and then loop the thread around the tip of the needle and pull it through.

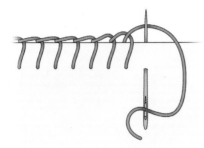

2 Take the next stitch the same way, making sure to keep the vertical stitches are all the same length and the same distance apart.

French knots

French knots make little beads of thread on the surface of the fabric.

1 Knot the thread and bring the needle up from the back of the fabric to the front. Wrap the thread once or twice around the tip of the needle, then push the needle into the fabric, right next to where it came up.

2 As you push the needle through, hold the wrapped threads tight against the fabric with the thumbnail of your other hand. Pull the needle all the way through so the wraps form a small knot on the surface of the fabric.

Straight stitch

Straight stitches are embroidery stitches similar to running stitch but worked as single stitches at different angles. They can be used to form other embroidery stitches, such as satin stitch and star stitch.

Satin stitch

Work straight stitches very close together, working to the outline of the shape and keeping the edges even. You may prefer to draw the shape onto the fabric first; if so, ensure that your stitches are worked to the outside of the line so it does not show.

Other techniques

Sewing on buttons

1 Mark the place where the button is to go.
Push the needle up through the fabric of
the shoe and sew a few stitches over and over
in the marked place to secure the thread end.

2 Bring the needle up through one of the holes in the
button and then back down through the second hole and
into the fabric of the shoe. Repeat this five or six times—don't
pull the thread too tight because there needs to be some room
between button and fabric. If there are four holes in the button,
use all four of them to make a cross pattern. Keep the stitches
close together under the middle of the button.

Sewing on beads and sequins

To stitch on a sequin with a bead, bring the thread up through the
fabric then thread on the sequin and tiny bead, take the thread
over the bead and back down through the hole in the sequin.
Single beads are sewn on in the same way, omitting the sequin.

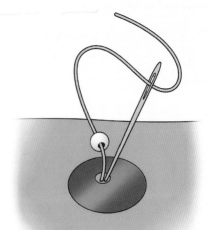

Tying a bow

Take hold of the middle of the ribbon and make a loop. Hold the loop with your
finger and thumb. With your left hand take the left side of the ribbon backward over
the top of your thumb. Now pull the ribbon through the loop you have made over
your thumb. Pull both loops of the bow firmly to make it secure.

Making fabric insoles

1 If you want to cover the insoles, place each shoe on the fabric and draw around the sole. Cut the fabric insoles out. Trim to fit inside the shoe.

2 Apply fabric glue over the insole of the shoe. Carefully place the new fabric insole inside the shoe over the original insole. Smooth into place and allow to dry before wearing the shoes.

Glueing

Glue guns

Many of these projects use a glue gun to fix embellishments in place. There are a number of different types of glue gun available on the market, although many of them will probably be too fancy and expensive for the projects featured in this book. I have always used a basic hot glue gun for arts and crafts; these usually come in a mini version and a standard size. The mini guns use smaller, thinner glue sticks but work in exactly the same way as the larger guns by heating up and melting the glue ready to apply. I usually use a glue gun that is mains-powered, but you can also buy battery-operated versions.

If you are concerned about the high temperatures reached by hot-melt glue guns, consider using a low-melt glue gun as an alternative. These use glue sticks that melt at much lower temperatures and although they do not produce quite such a strong bond as a hot-melt glue gun, they will be OK for most of the projects. Always use the correct glue sticks for the gun. Never use low-melt glue sticks in a hot-melt glue gun, because even the slightest pressure on the trigger can cause quite a lot of glue to squirt out.

All glue guns can get quite hot so I have a few safety tips to follow when using one to avoid any accidents.

- Always tie back long hair, roll up your sleeves, and pin back any loose clothing.

- Work on a large flat surface—such as a table—with good lighting, and have all the parts that need to be glued ready to hand.

- Be very careful to keep your fingers away from the nozzle.

- Use the trigger gently to release small amounts of glue at a time. If you are gluing something quite small, you may require some help from an adult.

Using the glue gun

Over the years I have learnt that it is best to leave a hot-melt glue gun to heat up for about 10–15 minutes before using, because it will not work effectively if the glue is not fully melted. Most glue guns have a little stand, either attached to the gun or supplied as a separate piece, so that you can stand it upright when you are not using it. It is important to use the stand because a glue gun can be ruined if it is left lying on its side—the glue may stick and harden onto the side of the gun in clumps, which stops fresh glue flowing down into the nozzle properly. A glue gun can also sometimes drip when it gets up to temperature, so you should put a piece of aluminum foil under the nozzle to catch drips and protect your work surface.

Using Bondaweb

Appliqué can be used to create motifs and surface decoration. Bondaweb is a quick and easy way to attach the layers together, keeping your design flat ready for further decorative stitching.

1 Trace the outlines of all the different pieces needed to make up the appliqué from the template. Transfer the shapes onto separate areas of the paper backing of a piece of Bondaweb.

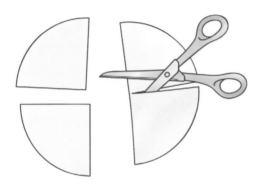

2 Cut the Bondaweb tracing into separate pieces. Decide on the color for each part of the design and select the fabrics.

3 Iron a Bondaweb piece onto the wrong side of the corresponding piece of fabric—you can place several pieces on the same fabric as long as they are spaced apart. Cut out the shape and peel off the paper backing of the Bondaweb.

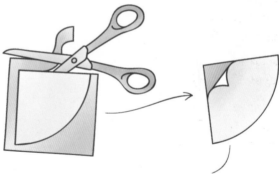

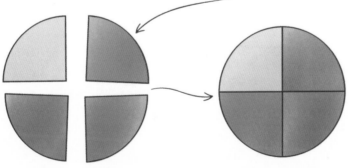

4 Arrange the pieces in their final position and iron in place.

Templates and copying

There are some templates provided in the back of this book to help you to make some of the projects more easily. The information with the template will say if you will need to enlarge it to make it the correct size. You must check this before starting to use the template.

Using templates

For some of the projects you will need to use the template to make a simple paper pattern to draw around.

1 Trace over the template onto a piece of tracing paper or greaseproof paper using a pencil, and then cut the shape out.

2 Place the paper pattern onto the fabric and draw around it. Cut the shape out of the fabric. If you are making pieces for appliqué, iron Bondaweb onto the back of the piece of fabric before cutting out the shape (see page 13).

3 For some of the projects you can trace the template directly onto Bondaweb. Place the smooth (paper side) of the Bondaweb facing upward over the template and use a pencil to draw over the design.

Cutting a stencil

There are two ways to make a stencil—if you have one, using the photocopier or the copying facility on a printer is the easiest. The second way is to use tracing paper to transfer the design onto the paper.

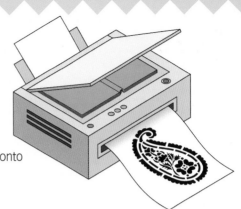

1 Photocopy the stencil design straight onto a piece of thick cartridge paper.

2 To trace the design, place the tracing paper over the image and carefully trace over all the lines using a soft pencil.

If you need to enlarge the template, either photocopy it at the percentage given or scan into a computer and print out at that percentage. For example, if the template must be enlarged by 200% then set the photocopier or scanner to this size before copying the image.

3 Then place the tracing paper onto a piece of cartridge paper with the pencil marks face downward. Re-draw over all the lines with a sharp hard pencil to transfer the design onto the paper.

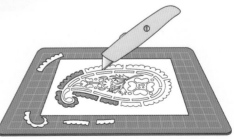

4 When the design is on the cartridge paper, use a craft knife and a cutting mat to cut out all the solid black shapes to make the stencil holes in the paper.

Choosing and caring

There are many different types of project featured within this book. Some can be made using old shoes, some require a fresh new pair, and some are made from scratch using fabric and other materials. In my opinion a lot of what makes a great design is down to the colors that are used and this is true for lots of the shoes I have designed in this book. Follow some of my simple guidelines to source or re-use shoes for your projects.

Cleaning and mending shoes

A pair of old shoes can often be upcycled to give them a new lease of life but you will need to prepare and clean them as much as possible before starting work. If you have a pair of plain old fabric sneakers, you can sometimes clean them by putting them through a medium cycle in the washing machine and they will come up looking and smelling really fresh. If you are unsure about doing this, then you can dissolve some detergent in a bowl of hot water and scrub the shoes with a nailbrush to get them clean again.

Another good tip for cleaning old shoes is to use nail varnish remover—this is great for getting rid of the scuffmarks that often occur on patent leather shoes. Colored nail varnish or a marker pen can also be used to disguise the odd little mark—be careful to match up the color first, and then lightly cover over any scrapes or marks to blend the color in.

If you are using nail varnish remover, nail varnish, or marker pens on your shoes, try them out on an inconspicuous place first to see the effect before using them on a part of the shoes that will show.

Sourcing cool shoes

If you are looking for a specific pair of shoes to customize or upcycle, you need to have a rough idea of what type of shoe you want and the color you would prefer. Before you begin, decide whether you are looking for a vibrant color or a more muted pale or pastel color and then on the general design of shoe.

Charity or thrift stores and yard sales are great places to look for pre-loved shoes but it can be quite time-consuming to go around all your local stores. If you have limited time, try one of the online auction sites. These sites allow you to narrow your search criteria so that you are looking for a specific style of shoe, size, and color. You can grab some real bargains, too!

Swapping is another good idea—your brothers, sisters, or friends might have a pair of shoes that they no longer like and want to swap—they may even just give them to you if they think they are going to a good cause. So don't be too shy to ask!

If you are searching for low-cost new shoes to embellish, check out some of the budget main street fashion shores—they often sell plain shoes that are very inexpensive and when you have transformed them they will be worth a lot more!

Looking after your shoes

If you want your shoes to last, it is important that you look after them both before and after you have decorated them. If your shoes are leather, buy a leather polish in a matching color and regularly polish them to keep them in the best condition possible. If you spill anything on fabric shoes, or your shoes become marked by mud, a wet cloth dipped in some washing powder or stain remover can often get rid of the mark instantly before it has time to soak into the fabric.

If you have decorated your shoes with sewn-on embellishments, sometimes the stitches will work loose over time. In this case, just refer back to the instructions in the book and re-sew the embellishment in place as soon as you see it that has become loose—don't wait until decorations are on the point of falling off, because you may lose them. If you double your thread before sewing, this makes the stitching even stronger, so it should stay in place for longer.

Remember always to check the manufacturer's instructions if you are using fabric paints and pens—some types may need you to iron over the colored areas after you have created the design, because this sets the paint or ink and stops it from fading or bleeding into surrounding areas if it gets wet.

Chapter 1

Flowers and fancies

Rosebud ballerina

Are you going to be a bridesmaid or flower girl? If so, these shoes will look absolutely beautiful and can be made in any color to match your dress. You could also cover the insole in pretty floral fabric, as we have done here.

You will need

- Candle
- 6 circles of pale pink silk fabric, each 2-in. (5-cm) diameter
- 6 circles of deep peach organza, each 1½-in. (4-cm) diameter
- 6 circles of deep pink organza, each 1¼-in. (3-cm) diameter
- 6 circles of pink organza, each ¾-in. (2-cm) diameter
- Scissors
- Needle and sewing thread
- Selection of pearl beads in different sizes
- Glue gun
- Satin ballet shoes in peach
- Fabric for insole (optional)
- Pencil (optional)
- PVA or fabric glue (optional)

1 Ask an adult to help you use a candle flame to seal the edges of the fabric circles by putting the edge very close to the flame—as you turn the circle around the fabric edge will distort slightly into an organic wavy edge.

2 Arrange the circles one on top of the other, with the biggest at the bottom and the smallest at the top. Work a couple of stitches through the center to hold all the circles in place and then slide a selection of pearl beads onto the thread and stitch in a cluster on top of the flower.

3 Use the glue gun to stick a rose onto the front of each ballet shoe. If you prefer, you can stitch the rose onto the shoe.

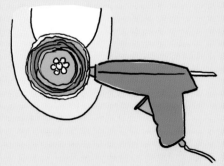

You will need some adult supervision for step 1, and for step 3 if using a glue gun.

4 To add a fabric insole to your shoes, choose a suitable fabric to go with your design and follow the instructions on page 11.

Flower sandals

If you are fed up with boring sandals and want to pretty them up a bit then follow these simple instructions to make a fabric flower. Your sandals will look gorgeous and perfect for a summer party, holiday evening, or wedding.

You will need

- 24 in. (60 cm) of pre-gathered or elasticized cotton or lace trim
- Scissors
- Thong sandals
- Glue gun
- Template on page 122
- 8 x 8 in. (20 x 20 cm) cream silk fabric
- Pins
- Needle and thread
- 20 in. (50 cm) silk ribbon
- 3¼ x 3¼ in. (8 x 8 cm) dusky pink silk fabric

1 Cut the length of trim in half and use a glue gun to stick it around the main part of the sandal.

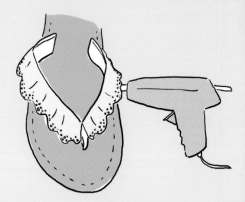

2 Use the template on page 122 to cut 10 petal shapes from the cream silk fabric. Fold and pin each of the petals lengthwise.

You may need some adult supervision for steps 1 and 4.

3 Work a running stitch along the curved raw edges of the folded petal and then continue along the next four petals so they are all stitched onto the same thread. Do not tie off the thread. Gather the petals along the thread as much as you can and then knot the thread to secure the petals in place.

4 Cut the ribbon in half and tie each length into a bow. Use the glue gun to fix the flower onto the center of the sandal strap and add the bow on top.

5 To finish the flower design with a rose, cut two more petals from the dusky pink silk. Work running stitch along the curved raw edge of one petal and slightly gather. Roll up the petal, flatten it with your fingers and then secure with a couple of hand stitches to hold the shape. Repeat with the other petal. Glue a rose into the center of each flower.

Flower power

This project shows you how to make pretty fabric flowers, which can easily be attached to any of your shoes. They are also great to put onto purses, bags, or hair bands and can be made in colors to match your outfit.

You will need

- 10 net circles, each approx. 2⅜ in. (6 cm) diameter

- 10 fabric circles, each approx. 2⅜ in. (6 cm) diameter

- Pins

- Needle and thread

- 10 small fabric circles, each approx. 1¾ in. (4.5 cm) diameter

- 24 in. (60 cm) net or lace ribbon

- Sequin shoes

- Fabric for insole (optional)

- Pencil (optional)

- PVA or fabric glue (optional)

1 Place five of the net circles on top of a corresponding fabric circle and then fold each pair in half with the net on the outside and pin.

2 Work a gathering stitch around the curved edge of the five semi-circles, stitching one after the other onto the same thread. Leave the needle attached and don't finish off the thread because you will need to pull the thread to gather the circles up.

3 Gather the petals on the thread and work them round into a circular flower. Tie the thread ends together to secure. Make a smaller flower in the same way—but without the net layer—from the five small fabric circles. Place the small flower on top of the big one and stitch in place.

4 Cut the length of net ribbon into four pieces each measuring 6 in. (15 cm). Take one piece and coil it up along one edge so that it looks a little bit like a rose. Stitch through the base several times to hold it in place then stitch it to the center of the flower.

5 Take another piece of net ribbon and loop it over three times, making a stitch to hold the ends in place. Position the ends behind the flower to one side and stitch in place. Repeat steps 1 to 5 to make the other flower.

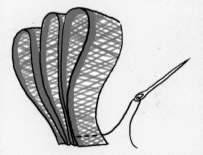

6 Position each flower as desired and stitch in place. To add a fabric insole to your shoes, choose a suitable fabric to go with your design and follow the instructions on page 11.

Matryoshka pumps

Don't you just love those nesting Russian dolls? If so, then have a go at these felt appliqué doll design pumps. Soooooo cute!

You will need

- Templates on page 123
- 3¼ x 1½ in. (8 x 4 cm) of white felt
- 3¼ x 1½ in. (8 x 4 cm) of yellow felt
- ¾ x 1½ in. (2 x 4 cm) of pink felt
- 3¼ x 1½ in. (8 x 4 cm) of dark red felt
- 4¾ x 2⅜ in. (12 x 6 cm) of patterned fabric backed onto felt using Bondaweb (see page 13)
- Scissors
- Pair of black ballet-style pumps
- Glue gun
- 20 in. (50 cm) teal blue rickrack
- Needle and embroidery floss in yellow and coral
- 2 lengths of red spotty ribbon, each ⅛ in. (3 mm) wide by 4 in. (10 cm)
- 4 pink sequins
- 2 purple buttons
- 32 in. (80 cm) yellow bias tape
- 4 yellow buttons
- 4 pink sparkly buttons
- 4 white sequins

1 Copy the templates and use them to cut out two face circles from white felt, two hair shapes from yellow felt, four cheek circles from pink felt, two collar pieces from dark red felt, and two headscarves from the patterned fabric backed with felt.

2 Glue the collar and then the headscarf pieces onto the front of each shoe using the glue gun. Cut the rickrack in half and add one piece around the edge of the appliqué design with the glue gun.

3 Embroider the hair piece onto the top of each face with little running stitches (see page 8) using yellow floss. Add French knots (see page 9) for each eye and then a couple of satin stitches to create a mouth in coral floss. Glue each face onto a shoe using the glue gun.

You may
need some adult
supervision for
steps 2, 3,
4, and 5.

4 Tie each length of red spotty ribbon into a bow (see page 10) and use the glue gun to stick one onto the hair of each doll. Add the pink cheeks, pink sequins, and the purple button in the same way.

5 Use the glue gun to stick the yellow bias tape onto the edge of the shoe. The best way to do this is to stick the outer edge down first all the way around and then apply glue to the edge inside, fold the bias tape over and stick it down inside. Add the buttons around the front of each shoe to complete.

Velvet and lace

There are so many ways of making flower decorations but I really love this technique—it's such a simple idea but looks so pretty and effective. These pumps would be beautiful with your poshest frock for a special occasion.

You will need

- 30 strips of peach velvet ribbon, each 3¼ in. (8 cm) long
- Needle and thread
- Two pieces of tulle netting, each measuring 2⅜ x 12 in. (6 x 30 cm)
- Scissors
- Lace flower
- Pair of plain pumps
- Glue gun

1 Tie a knot in the center of each of the lengths of velvet ribbon. Fold each length in half with wrong sides together so the raw ends meet.

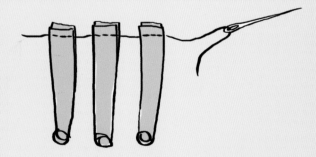

2 Work a stitch through the raw ends of the first length and then continue straight onto the next one, repeating this step until half the knotted ribbons are stitched onto the same thread.

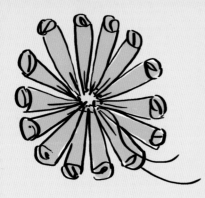

3 Pull the thread tight to bring the ribbons round into a circle and tie both ends of the sewing thread into a knot to secure.

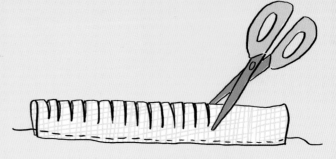

4 Fold one piece of tulle netting over along its length and work a gathering stitch along the raw edges, leaving the needle in place at the end without fastening off. Snip into the netting every ¼ in. (0.5 cm) all the way along the folded edge, being careful not to cut as far as the stitching.

5 Pull on the thread to gather the flower up and tie both ends of thread together to secure. Stitch the tulle flower onto the velvet flower and then add a lace flower into the center to complete the decoration.

My lace flower was a motif cut from a piece of lace fabric.

You may need some adult supervision for step 6

6 Repeat steps 2 to 5 to make the second flower. Use the glue gun to stitck each flower and lace embellishment onto the front of one of the shoes.

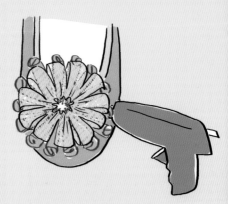

Upcycled zippers

Old metal zippers can make brilliant decorations for shoes—you can cut them out of unwanted clothing. Follow these easy steps to make fantastic coiled embellishments that will transform a plain pair of shoes into a real talking point.

You will need

- Long black metal zipper
- Long red metal zipper
- Scissors
- Needle and thread
- Pair of black pointed-toe pumps
- Glue gun
- Fabric for insole (optional)
- Pencil (optional)
- PVA or fabric glue (optional)

1 Take the black zipper and cut off the bottom just above the zipper stop so that the two sides will come apart completely. Repeat on the red zipper so that you have four lengths.

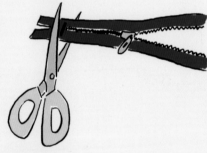

2 Work running stitch down the length of one of the black zipper pieces but do not finish off at the end. Pull the thread to gather each zipper along the line of stitching until it begins to coil into loops. When you are happy with the amount of coil, secure the thread with a couple of little stitches to stop the gathers coming undone. Repeat on the other black zipper piece for the other shoe.

3 Repeat step 2 with the red zippers, but gather one end of these a little more to make a tight coil that looks like a rose. Secure the rose shape with a couple of small stitches and gather the rest of the zipper into loops. When you are happy with the design, secure the thread end with a couple of little stitches to stop the gathers coming undone.

The length of zipper you need depends on how big you want the decorations.

You may need some adult supervision for step 4.

4 Use a glue gun to stick the zipper decorations onto the front of the shoe—it might be a good idea to plan out how you would like them to look before you start sticking them in place. To add a fabric insole to your shoes, choose a suitable fabric to go with your design and follow the instructions on page 11.

Roses 'n' bows

Espadrilles are the perfect comfortable summer shoe but can sometimes seem a little plain—so why not add a touch of embellishment with this pretty ribbon rose technique.

You will need

- Approx. 11 in. (28 cm) of crochet trim
- Pair of floral espadrilles
- Scissors
- Needle and thread
- Large eyed needle (bodkin)
- Silk ribbon in three coordinating colors
- 6 buttons, two in each color
- Beads and sequins
- 2 small bows

1 Cut the crochet trim in half and hand stitch one strip onto the shoe across the top front. Repeat on the other shoe.

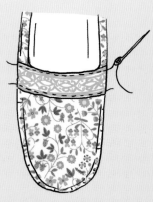

2 Work three star stitches on the upper outside front of the first shoe using sewing thread—each star should have five stitches/points. Repeat on the other shoe.

3 Thread the bodkin needle with one of the silk ribbons and work the needle under and over the star stitches, starting at the center and working outward to make a rose. Snip the ribbon as you finish the rose and use a normal needle and thread to secure the end into the shoe fabric. Repeat this step to make three roses on each shoe.

4 Stitch a few coordinating buttons and beads around the roses. Stitch a small bow onto each shoe to complete the design.

Chapter 2

Sequins and sparkles

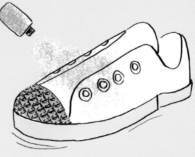

Buttons 'n' bows

Buttons are such a thrifty and easy way to change the look of a pair of shoes and very simple to apply. Raid your button jar, find a selection of pretty buttons, and you're ready to go!

You will need

- Selection of buttons (approx. 11 for each shoe)
- Pair of pumps
- Glue gun
- 20 in. (50 cm) of dotted ribbon
- Fabric for insole (optional)
- Pencil (optional)
- PVA or fabric glue (optional)

1 Arrange the buttons onto the front of the shoes—color is very important with this, choose your buttons carefully with a limited number of colors (3 or 4). A good selection of shapes and sizes will make the design look more interesting.

2 When you are happy with the design, use the glue gun to stick each button in the desired place.

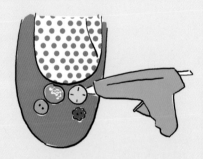

3 Cut the ribbon in half and tie each half into a bow (see page 10). Glue a bow onto each shoe, using the photograph as a guide for position.

4 To add a fabric insole to your shoes, choose a suitable fabric to go with your design and follow the instructions on page 11.

You may need some adult supervision for steps 2 and 3.

Rhinestones and ribbons

You can add a little bit of sparkle to any shoes with easy-to-use hot-fix rhinestones. This project shows you how to use the hot-fix tool to transform a pair of sneakers—ours are floral but the rhinestones look great on plain sneakers, too.

You will need

- Floral sneakers
- Hot-fix rhinestones
- Tweezers (optional)
- Hot-fix tool with the correct size attachment for your rhinestones
- 1¾ yd (1.5 m) of lilac ribbon
- Clear sticky tape

1 Remove the original laces from the sneakers. Pick up a rhinestone (you may need to use tweezers), place it in the desired position and then hold the tip of the hot-fix tool on the rhinestone, following the manufacturer's instructions, until it is secure. Repeat until you have applied rhinestones all over the shoe.

2 Cut the ribbon in half. Roll the last ½ in. (1 cm) of the ribbon at each end and tightly wrap a piece of clear sticky tape around to seal the ends. This will make it easier to thread the ribbon laces through the holes.

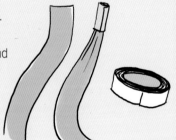

You may need some adult supervision for step 1.

3 Thread the ribbon through the lace holes in your desired threading pattern. Put the sneakers on and tie the ribbon in a pretty bow (see page 10).

Be careful when using the hot fix tool—the end must be very hot to melt the glue on the rhinestones.

Bling-bling rosette peep-toes

Bright coral is such a trendy color at the moment and it goes hand in hand with a bit of bling. A pair of sparkly earrings just adds the finishing touch to these eye-catching open-toe shoes.

You will need

- 2 circles of pink felt, each 3½ in. (9 cm) in diameter
- 2 circles of Bondaweb, each 3½ in. (9 cm) in diameter
- 2 circles of coral/peach silk, each 3½ in. (9 cm) in diameter
- Iron
- Needle and thread
- Scissors
- Pinking shears
- 64 in. (160 cm) of coral lace trim
- Coral peep-toe pumps
- Glue gun
- Pair of sparkly clip earrings
- Fabric for insole (optional)
- Pencil (optional)
- PVA or fabric glue (optional)

1 To make the rosette, first stick a felt circle to a silk circle with wrong sides together using Bondaweb, following the manufacturer's instructions (see page 13). Work running stitch around the raw edge of the bonded circle.

2 With the silk side facing up, pull on the thread ends to gather the edge inward to make a yo-yo (Suffolk puff) with the silk fabric on the inside. Tie both ends of the sewing thread together to secure the yo-yo.

3 Make a snip into the flat back of the yo-yo and cut away the back near the edge all round, using a pair of pinking shears. This will give you a gathered silk rosette flower. Repeat steps 1 to 3 to make the second rosette.

You may need some adult supervision for steps 1, 5, and 6.

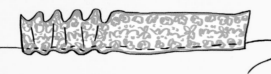

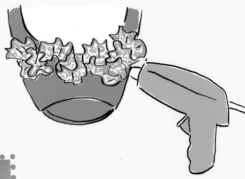

4 Cut the lace trim into two equal pieces. Work a
   gathering stitch down the first length and then
pull on the needle to gather the lace and manipulate
it into a spiral shape. Secure the end of the thread
with a couple of stitches. Repeat with the other
length of lace.

5 Use a glue gun to stick the
   lace around the front top
edge of each shoe, twisting the
lace into a spiral shape as you go.

6 Glue the rosette onto the
   center of each shoe and
then glue an earring on top. If you
want to add a fabric insole, follow
the instructions on page 11.

St Tropez style

This is a quick and easy way to customize boring old sandals into something stylish enough for the Côte d'Azur. All you need are a few lengths of yarn, a pair of chandelier-style earrings, and a couple of covered buttons.

You will need

- 2 lengths of yarn in each of three coordinating colors, each length measuring 120 in. (3 m)

- Pencil

- Pair of sandals

- Glue gun

- Pair of chandelier-style earrings

- 2 self-cover buttons

- Scraps of fabric

- Scissors

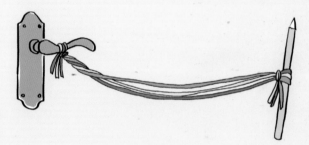

1 To make the twisted cord, take one set (3 lengths, one in each color) of yarn and tie together at one end to a door handle. Tie the other ends together to a pencil. Holding the pencil, pull the yarn tight, turn to your right and begin to spin the pencil with your right hand whilst holding the yarn with your left hand. Spin until the yarn is starting to twist back on itself.

You may need some adult supervision for steps 3 and 4.

2 You will need someone to help you here. Ask your helper to take hold of the middle of the twisted cord while you walk over to the door handle, keeping the yarn tight at all times, until both ends are next to one another and the cord is doubled. Now take hold of the middle of the cord and ask your helper to remove the cord from the door handle but keep tight hold of both ends. Begin to work your way toward your helper, pinching the yarn along the way—it will twist itself together to form a twisted cord. Knot the ends to stop it from unwinding.

3 Position the twisted cord into a design that you like and fix it to the sandal straps using the glue gun. Remove the hanging hooks from the earrings and discard. Use the hot glue gun to stick the earrings onto the central area of the sandal strap. Repeats steps 1 to 3 for the other sandal.

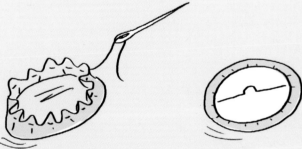

4 Cut two circles of fabric approx. ⅝ in. (1.5 cm) larger than the diameter of the button and work running stitch around the edge, leaving the needle still attached at the end. Gather the circle slightly and insert the front of the self-cover button, then gather the fabric fully and tie off. Push the back of the button on until you hear it "click" into place. Glue the fabric button into the center of the earring using the glue gun.

Art deco feathers

Feathers are brilliant for glamming up a pair of ordinary shoes. These feathers were taken from an old pair of earrings but you can buy decorative feathers from many sewing notion or craft stores.

You will need

- Pair of large circular earrings
- Glue gun
- Pair of nude color ballet pumps
- 6 small feathers, to make up two matching sets
- 2 large black gems or beads
- 2 short lengths of chain
- Fabric for insole (optional)
- Pencil (optional)
- PVA or fabric glue (optional)

You may need some adult supervision for steps 1, 2, and 3.

1 Use the glue gun to attach a circular earring to the front of each shoe. Make sure you position the earrings as a mirror image for a matching pair of shoes.

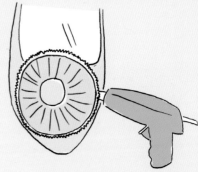

2 Arrange three feathers on the earring to one side and use the glue gun to stick them in place. Repeat on the other shoe.

My earring had a hole near the center so I glued around the outside edge only and inserted the feather ends under the edge of the hole.

3 Use the hot glue gun to add the black gems or beads and the chain as extra embellishment, using the photograph as a guide.

4 To add a fabric insole to your shoes, choose a suitable fabric to go with your design and follow the instructions on page 11.

Adapt this design to suit the shape of different earrings.

Studs 'n' glitter

These stud and glitter sneakers will certainly make you stand out in a crowd. They are really fun to make and great if your sneakers are starting to look a bit old and worn—you can give them a whole new lease of life!

You will need

- Pair of canvas sneakers
- Gold hot-fix studs
- Hot-fix tool
- Masking tape
- Newspaper
- Mod Podge glue
- Brush
- Gold glitter
- Two lengths of black ribbon for the laces
- Fabric for insole (optional)
- Pencil (optional)
- PVA or fabric glue (optional)

1 Remove the laces from the sneakers. Use the hot-fix tool to attach the gold studs onto the toe panel of each shoe. Start at the top of the panel and work across and downward in lines until the area is completely covered.

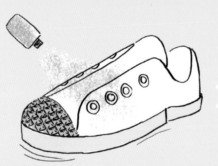

You may need some adult supervision for step 1.

2 Tape over the white rubber sole with masking tape to stop any glitter sticking to this area. Apply Mod Podge to the canvas of the sneaker and then sprinkle on the glitter until the shoe is completely covered. Repeat on the other shoe.

3 Let dry until the glitter has stuck then shake the shoes to get rid of any excess. Check the glitter is even, adding more Mod Podge and glitter to any areas that are not covered well enough. Leave both shoes to dry completely. To protect the glitter, use the Mod Podge as a varnish, painting a thin layer over the top of the glitter. Leave the shoes to dry.

4 Lace a length of black ribbon through each set of eyelet holes in your chosen pattern. To add a fabric insole to your shoes, choose a suitable fabric to go with your design and follow the instructions on page 11.

Chapter 3

Animal magic

Dinosaur slippers

If you want to improve or practice your sewing machine skills then this project is great for you. If you are not so good on the sewing machine then ask an adult to help you with the machine while you do the cutting and hand sewing.

You will need

- Slipper templates on pages 120 and 121
- 12 x 8 in. (30 x 20 cm) of bright green fleece
- 10 x 8 in. (25 x 20 cm) of light green fleece
- 10 x 8 in. (25 x 20 cm) of curtain lining
- 8 x 6 in. (20 x 15 cm) of green-brown felt
- Pencil
- Scissors
- Sewing machine and thread
- Fiberfill stuffing
- Needle and thread
- 4 x 1¼ in. (3 cm) circles of white felt (outer eye template on page 120)
- 4 x ½ in. (1 cm) circles of red felt (inner eye template on page 120)
- Pins
- 2 strips of white felt, each 4¾ x 1¼ in. (12 x 3 cm)
- 2 strips of light green fleece, each 6 x 3¼ in. (15 x 8 cm)

1 Copy the templates and use to cut four slipper uppers from bright green fleece, two soles from light green fleece, and two from the curtain lining. You will need to reverse the templates for half the pieces so you have matching pairs of uppers and soles. Cut 12 triangles from the green-brown felt.

2 To make the spikes, place two triangles together and machine stitch along two edges. Trim back the seams. Turn the felt inside out and stuff with fiberfill. Repeat to make all six spikes.

You may need some adult supervision for steps 2, 3, 6, 7, and 8.

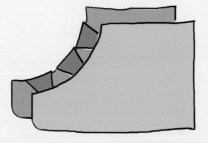

3 To make the upper of the slipper take two of the upper pieces and place them right sides together. Insert three of the triangles between the two layers as shown. Machine stitch along the top curved center front seam only, trapping the triangles in place at the same time. Trim the seam and turn the upper right side out. Repeat for the other upper.

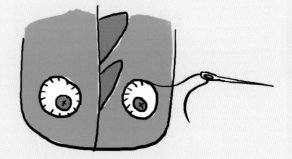

4 Pin the white and red circles onto the front of each slipper as shown and blanket stitch (see page 9) around the edge to keep them in place. Turn inside out.

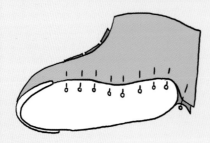

5 Place the curtain lining underneath the light green sole then pin the upper of the slipper to the sole and lining, with right sides facing. The upper will not fit around the sole exactly—follow the shape of the sole as closely as possible and then trim off any excess upper sticking out on either side at the front. Insert the white felt strip for the teeth between the sole and upper along the front seam and pin in place.

6 Machine stitch around the sole starting at the center back and working all the way around (the back upper seam is still open at this point). Turn right side out and check everything has caught in place. Turn the slipper inside out again stitch up the upper back seam. Trim the seams and turn the slipper right side out. Repeat steps 5 and 6 for the other slipper.

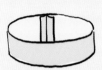

7 Fold each strip of light green fleece over widthwise and machine stitch the short back seam. Trim the seams and turn both rings right way out.

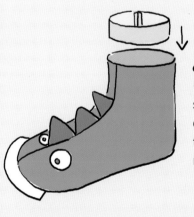

8 Insert one ring right into the top of each slipper, with right side facing the wrong side of the slipper, so the upper edge of the ring lines up with the top edge of the slipper. Pin and machine stitch around the top of the slipper just down from the edge. Turn the contrast ring out over the top edge of each slipper and press.

9 To finish, cut the white felt at the front into scary teeth shapes.

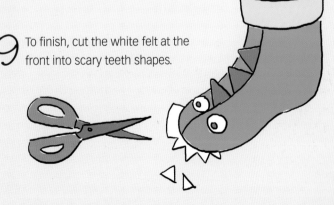

Pussy-cat bows

Transform a simple plain pair of black Mary Jane pumps into cute little cats with just a tiny amount of felt, glue, and ribbon—it couldn't be easier!

You will need

- Cat templates on page 120
- 2⅜-in. (6-cm) square of pink felt for ears and nose
- 1½-in. (4-cm) square of white felt
- 2-in. (5-cm) square of green felt
- 1½-in. (4-cm) square of black felt
- Scissors
- Glue gun
- Black canvas Mary Jane pumps
- 6 in. (15 cm) pink rickrack braid
- Needle and white embroidery floss
- 12 in. (30 cm) narrow pink ribbon
- Stick-on rhinestones or sequins
- Fabric for insole (optional)
- Pencil (optional)
- PVA or fabric glue (optional)

1 Use the templates to cut out four outer ears and two noses from pink felt, four inner ears from white felt, four eyes from green felt, and four inner eyes from black felt. Using the photograph as a guide, position the pieces onto the front of each shoe and use a glue gun to attach them in place.

2 Cut the rickrack into two lengths and stick one length over the top of each shoe front, just below the ears, using the glue gun.

You may
need some adult
supervision for
steps 1, 2, and 4.

3 Using white embroidery floss, make a series of straight stitches for whiskers, eyelashes, and around the inner ear. If your shoes are canvas you should be able to stitch right through the shoe.

4 Cut the length of pink ribbon into two pieces and tie each piece into a bow (see page 10). Use the glue gun to stick the bow onto the shoe, using the photograph as a guide for position.

5 Add a rhinestone to the center of each eye and under the ear on the other side to the bow. If your rhinestones are not the stick-on type or you want to use sequins instead, use the glue gun to fix them in place.

6 To add a fabric insole to your shoes, choose a suitable fabric to go with your design and follow the instructions on page 11.

Little white mice

Keep these little white mouse pumps away from the cat pumps on page 60 or there will be trouble! Adapt the basic idea to make other cute animals too.

You will need

- Mouse templates on page 120
- 2⅜-in. (6-cm) square of pink felt
- 1½-in. (4-cm) square of white felt
- Pencil
- Scissors
- Needle and pink embroidery floss
- Fabric glue or PVA
- Pair of white pumps
- Approx. 6 in (15 cm) of white lace trim
- 2 crochet flower motifs
- 2 small blue ribbon bows
- 4 black sequins
- 4 black rhinestones
- Pink wool
- Large eye needle
- Fabric for insole (optional)

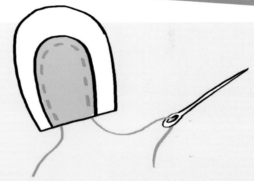

1 Copy the templates and use to cut out four inner ears and two noses from pink felt and four outer ears from white felt. Place an inner ear on each outer ear and hand sew together using a small running stitch. Using the photograph as a guide, position the ears onto the front of each shoe and either sew or glue them in place.

Canvas pumps are easier to sew than leather or faux leather—if you need to stitch these use a denim needle, which is very sharp—you may need to ask an adult to help.

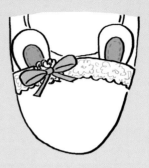

2 Cut the lace trim in half. Use the fabric glue to attach a strip of lace across the top at the front of each shoe, just below the ears. Stick a crochet flower and a blue ribbon bow onto the lace trim of each shoe.

3 Stitch or glue two black sequins onto the front of each shoe for the eyes and add a black rhinestone on top of each sequin. Glue a pink nose onto each shoe using the photograph as a guide for position.

4 Thread the large eye needle with the pink wool and stitch three long straight stitches on each side of the nose for the whiskers, sewing through the front of the shoe. Repeat on the other shoe.

You may need some adult supervision for step 4.

5 To add a fabric insole to your shoes, choose a suitable fabric to go with your design and follow the instructions on page 11.

Monster slippers

This is another project to practice and improve your sewing machine skills, but you can ask an adult to help you with the machine stitching while you do all the fun cutting and hand sewing.

You will need

- Slipper templates on page 121
- 24 x 16 in. (60 x 40 cm) of dotted pink fleece
- 10 x 8 in. (25 x 20 cm) of pink felt
- Scissors
- Sewing machine and thread
- 10-in. (25-cm) square of Bondaweb
- Tape measure
- Iron
- 8 x 10 in. (20 x 25 cm) of purple felt
- Pencil
- 6½ x 12 in. (16 x 30 cm) of floral jersey fabric
- Needle and white embroidery floss
- 4 white sequins
- 4 small pink seed beads
- Pins
- 16 in. (40 cm) of green ribbon

1 Use the slipper templates to cut four slipper uppers from dotted pink fleece, two soles from dotted pink fleece, and two soles from pink felt. You will need to reverse the templates for half the pieces so you have matching pairs of uppers and soles.

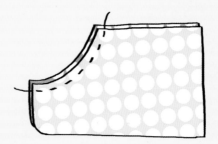

2 To make the upper of the slipper, take a pair of upper pieces and place them right sides together. Machine stitch along the top curved center front seam, then trim the seam and turn the upper right side out. Repeat for the other slipper.

You may need some adult supervision for steps 2, 5, 8, and 9.

Materials and templates are for slippers to fit US size 2.5 (UK size 2) —you may need to adjust them for other sizes.

3 Cut a 2-in. (5-cm) wide strip off one side of the Bondaweb and set aside. Iron the larger piece of Bondaweb onto the back of the purple felt, following the manufacturer's instructions (see page 13). On the paper backing, using the templates on page 121, draw four of the larger circles plus six triangles and four leaf shapes. Cut a 2-in. (5-cm) wide strip off one short end of the floral jersey fabric and iron the smaller piece of Bondaweb onto the back. Draw four of the smaller circles on the paper backing.

4 Cut out the four felt and four floral circles. Remove the paper backing from the floral circles and iron one on top of each felt circle. Remove the paper backing from the felt circles, and iron two onto each slipper upper as eyes, using the photograph as a guide. Cut out the six triangles, remove the paper backing and position them onto the slipper fronts as shown in the photograph. Iron to fix in place. Using white embroidery floss, work back stitch around the edge of each floral circle and then add three straight stitches at the top edge of each for eyelashes. Stitch a sequin with a bead on top into the center of each eye.

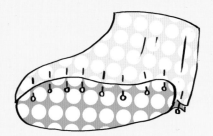

5 Place a felt sole onto the wrong side of a dotted pink fleece sole and then pin a slipper upper to the sole with right side facing the felt. The upper will not fit around the sole exactly—follow the shape of the sole as closely as possible and then trim off any excess upper sticking out on either side at the front. Machine stitch around the sole starting at the center back and working all the way around (the back seam of the upper is still open at this point).

6 Turn the slipper right side out and check everything has caught in place, then turn wrong side out again and trim back the seams. With the slippers still wrong out stitch the back seam of the upper. Trim the seam and turn the slipper right side out. Repeat steps 5 and 6 for the other slipper.

7 Cut out the four leaf shapes from the Bondaweb-backed felt and remove the paper backing. Iron two leaf shapes onto the front of each slipper using the photograph as a guide for position.

8 Cut the strip of floral jersey fabric in half along its length. Fold each strip over widthwise and machine stitch down the short back seam to make two rings. Trim the seam and turn both rings right side out.

9 Insert one ring right into the top of each slipper, with right side facing the wrong side of the slipper, so the upper edge of the ring lines up with the top edge of the slipper. Pin and machine stitch around the top of the slipper just down from the edge. Turn the contrast ring out over the top edge of each slipper and press.

10 Cut the green ribbon in half. Tie each length into a bow and stitch one onto the upper band of each slipper.

Chapter 4

Fabric and ribbons

Braided roses

If you quickly want to change the look of a pair of sandals, or maybe make them match an outfit, follow these instructions for a super speedy way to do just that!

You will need

- 6 strips of soft floaty fabric, each 60 x 2⅜ in. (150 x 6 cm)
- Glue gun
- Pair of thong sandals with ankle strap removed

1 Place three strips of the fabric together at one end (one piece on top of the other) with a dab of glue between layers. Apply glue to the toe post of the sandal and carefully wrap the fabric ends round it until they are secure. Allow to dry.

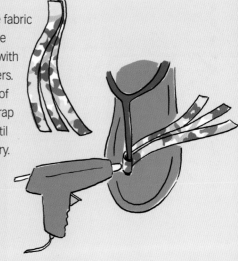

2 Braid the fabric strips over the main bar of the sandal to completely cover it. You will need to wrap two of the lengths of fabric under the bar and one over as you are braiding to secure the braid to the bar.

3 When you get to the end of the main bar, take one strip of fabric to each side and leave one in the middle. Use the glue gun to stick the side fabric strips onto the side straps of the sandal, leaving the ends loose so they can be tied around the ankle.

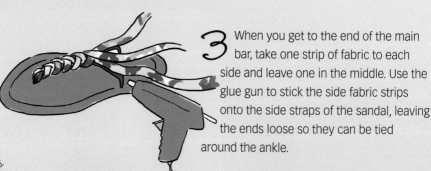

You may need some adult supervision for steps 1, 3, and 4.

4 Twist the central strip of fabric and hold in one hand. Apply glue to the center of the main bar and curl the fabric strip around in a circle to create a rose design. When you feel your rose is big enough, trim off the remaining length of fabric.

Loopy flip-flops

This thrifty project is great to use up scraps of ribbon and lace to create a vibrant pair of flip-flops that will be perfect on vacation!

You will need

- Selection of ribbons and old zippers
- Scissors
- Rickrack braid
- Glue gun
- Flip-flops
- Netting
- Needle and thread
- Beads and buttons

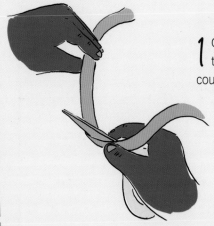

1 Curl the ribbon by pulling it over the edge of the scissor blades a couple of times.

2 Twist a length of ribbon, rickrack, or zipper around into loops and use the glue gun to stick it to the flip-flop strap. Keep adding pieces until the strap is completely covered—the design should look busy and loopy.

3 Cut a piece of netting approx. 4 in. (10 cm) long and work a line of running stitch along the center, leaving the needle attached at the end. Pull the needle to gather the netting and secure with a couple of stitches. Make two or three more in the same way and use the glue gun to attach them to the flip-flop strap.

4 Glue beads and buttons onto the strap to fill any remaining gaps or to add more color to the design. Repeat all the steps on the other flip-flop.

Sparkly lace and pearls

These lace-covered shoes are so pretty; they would be great to wear if you are going to be a bridesmaid. If you don't like heels, simply use the same technique on a flat pair of shoes.

You will need

- PVA glue
- Pair of heeled shoes
- Oddments of lace
- Scissors
- Pearl beaded lace motifs
- 2 sparkly brooches
- Glue gun
- Fabric for insole (optional)
- Pencil (optional)
- PVA or fabric glue (optional)

1 Apply glue to an area of the shoe. Cut a piece of lace approximately the same size as the area you have glued and position the lace onto it. Hold for a few seconds while the glue becomes tacky and then trim the lace back to fit the shape of the shoe neatly.

2 Repeat step 1 all the way over the shoe until it is completely covered in lace. If you are using a piece of lace that has no hemmed edges then you will need to turn it under along the top edge of the shoes for a neat finish.

3 Cut two lace motifs out of the beaded lace and use the glue gun to stick these in place around the toe area of each shoe.

You may need some adult supervision for steps 3 and 4

If you are using a lace top with a hemmed edge, line up the hem with the top edge of the shoe for a nice tidy finish.

I started at the back with an area about 4 in. (10 cm) long and worked forward. Cut small pieces for more tricky areas.

4 Use the glue gun to stick a brooch into the center of the toe area on each shoe. To add a fabric insole to your shoes, choose a suitable fabric to go with your design and follow the instructions on page 11.

Woven crochet pumps

Crochet shoes are a fantastic base to work onto—they offer the perfect fabric to weave through. This is a really simple project that is perfect for beginners!

You will need

- Large-eyed needle (bodkin)
- Selection of yarns, trims, and threads in coordinating colors
- Pair of crochet fabric shoes
- Fabric glue or PVA
- 2 lengths of silk fabric, each 2½ x 6½ in. (6.5 x 16.5 cm)
- Sewing needle and thread
- Fabric for insole (optional)
- Pencil (optional)

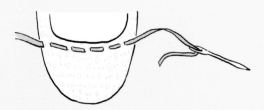

1 Thread up the bodkin with any of the yarns and weave it over the front of the shoe (start at the top) in and out of the crochet. When you have completed a line of stitching, change the yarn and continue with further lines working downward in different colors. Leave a tail of yarn at the beginning and end of each line.

2 Weave a line of trimming all the way around the opening of the shoe to continue the design. Snip off all the yarn ends and use a dab of fabric glue to secure them in place.

3 To make the bow, fold under the top and bottom edge of the silk and press in place. With the flat side facing up, take hold of the silk and loop the right-hand end underneath about one third of the way and secure with a couple of stitches.

4 Loop under the other side to match in size (which will leave a long end free) and scrunch the bow in at the center. Take a couple of stitches through the center to secure the bow. Take the long end over the center of the bow and to the back and stitch it in place.

5 Use fabric glue to stick the bow onto the shoes, or stitch in place. To add a fabric insole to your shoes, choose a suitable fabric to go with your design and follow the instructions on page 11.

Big bows

This project is a little more advanced but is great if you want to develop your machine stitching skills further. These slippers can be made in your favorite fabric and are great to slip into a suitcase when you go on vacation.

You will need

- Slipper sole template on page 122
- 12 x 26 in. (30 x 65 cm) of floral fabric
- Scissors
- Pencil
- 10 x 8 in. (25 x 20 cm) of white felt
- 10 x 8 in. (25 x 20 cm) of fleece
- 12 x 17½ in. (30 x 44 cm) of striped fabric
- Sewing machine and thread
- Pins
- Sewing needle and basting thread
- 48 in. (120 cm) of bias binding
- 10 x 8 in. (25 x 20 cm) of Bondaweb
- Iron

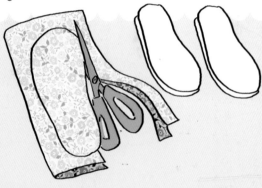

1 Copy the sole template and reduce or enlarge it on the photocopier to fit the size of your foot. Cut a 10 x 8 in. (25 x 20 cm) piece of floral fabric, fold it in half and place the sole template on top. Draw around it and cut out the shape through both layers (this will create a right and left foot). Fold the felt and the fleece in half and cut a sole out of each through both layers. You will now have three sole pieces for each slipper; one fabric, one felt, and one fleece.

Materials and templates are for slippers to fit up to US size 7.5 (UK size 5) —you may need to adjust them for other sizes.

2 Cut the striped fabric into four pieces each 6 x 8¾ in. (15 x 22 cm) and cut four pieces the same size from the remaining floral fabric. Place a striped piece and a floral piece right sides together and machine stitch around three sides leaving one short side open. Trim seams, turn right side out, and press. Repeat to create a total of four bow pieces.

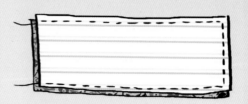

3 To construct the slipper, take a matching fleece and felt sole and place the fleece right side up on top of the felt. Position a bow piece on top on either side with the raw open edges in line with the edge of the slipper. Pin everything in place and baste, then remove the pins.

4 Pin a length of bias binding all round the edge of each slipper to encase the raw edges of all layers. Pin and baste the binding in place, then remove the pins. Machine along the bias binding through all layers using a zigzag stitch and keeping the stitching toward the inner edge of the binding.

You may need some adult supervision for step 5.

5 Fold the Bondaweb in half and use the sole template to cut two pieces. Trim each piece down around the edges by approx. ¼ in. (0.5 cm) and then iron one onto the reverse of each fabric sole, following the manufacturer's instructions (see page 13). Peel away the paper backing and iron a fabric sole on top of the fleece on each slipper, making sure it covers the zigzag stitching.

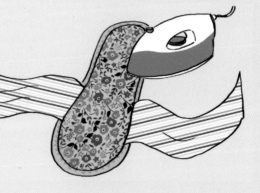

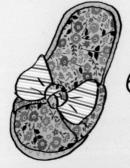

6 Put your feet onto the slippers and tie the fabric ends into a bow on each slipper to finish.

Night owl

These are super quick and easy customized slippers! All you need is a pair of inexpensive spa slippers, some fabric, Bondaweb, and bias binding. This would be a great idea for a sleepover party—you could all make your own pair of cute slippers!

You will need

- 14 x 10 in. (35 x 25 cm) of owl design fabric
- 10 x 8 in. (25 x 20 cm) of Bondaweb
- Iron
- Pair of spa slippers
- Pencil
- Fabric scissors
- Pins
- 20 in. (50 cm) of bias tape
- Needle and matching thread
- 4 small pearl buttons
- 4 small beads

1 Cut a piece of fabric about 10 in. (25 cm) high by 8 in. (20 cm) wide for the insoles. Apply the Bondaweb onto the wrong side of the fabric using an iron and following the manufacturer's instructions (see page 13). Fold the fabric in half along its length, place the spa slipper onto it and draw around it. Cut out the shape.

2 You now have a pair of pieces. Trim the shapes if necessary to fit over the insoles of the slippers. Peel off the paper backing of the Bondaweb and iron to fix a fabric piece onto the insole of each slipper.

You may need some adult supervision for step 2.

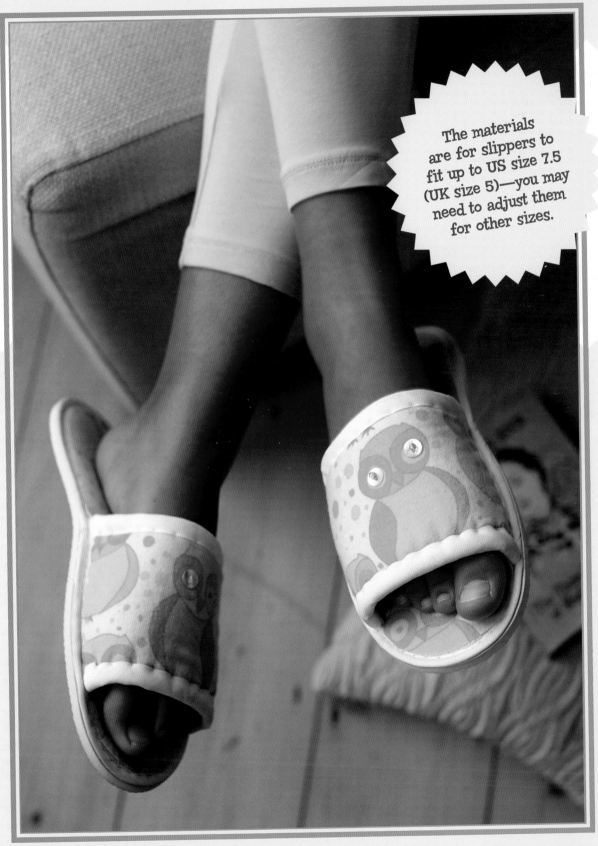

The materials are for slippers to fit up to US size 7.5 (UK size 5)—you may need to adjust them for other sizes.

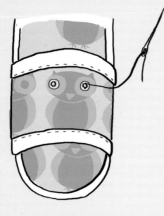

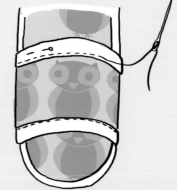

3 Measure the slipper upper and add ⅝ in. (1.5 cm) to each side and each end. Use these measurements to draw two rectangles on the fabric to cover the uppers, making sure that one of the owl motifs will be right in the center of each rectangle. Cut the rectangles out. Place one onto each slipper upper, tuck the top, bottom, and side edges under to neaten and pin in place.

4 Cut a length of bias tape to fit the front edge of each slipper upper with approx. ⅜ in. (1 cm) extra at each end. Turn under the end to neaten and then wrap the binding around the front edge of each slipper upper, removing the previous pins and re-pinning as you go. Repeat to bind the back edge of each upper.

5 Work small running stitches along the bias tape right through all layers to stitch the binding in place. Stitch a button with a bead on top over each owl eye for further decoration.

Hippy dippy

This is the perfect opportunity to experiment with color. A plain pair of cotton fabric shoes can be totally transformed with a packet of dye, some elastic bands, household bleach, and your imagination!

You will need

- Packet of dye
- Plastic bowl or container
- Warm water
- Plastic gloves
- Plastic sheets or newsprint
- Paintbrush
- Pair of cotton espadrilles
- 8 x 8 in. (20 x 20 cm) of white cotton fabric
- Elastic bands
- Bleach
- Popsicle stick
- Pencil
- PVA or fabric glue

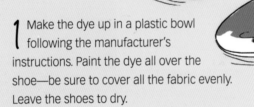

1 Make the dye up in a plastic bowl following the manufacturer's instructions. Paint the dye all over the shoe—be sure to cover all the fabric evenly. Leave the shoes to dry.

Wear plastic gloves when working with dye and cover the work area with plastic sheet or newsprint. Be careful not to get dye on other fabrics.

You may need some adult supervision for steps 1, 3, and 4.

2 Gather up a small area of the piece of cotton fabric into a small bunch and tie an elastic band very tightly around the base. Repeat all over the fabric until it is covered in gathered bunches.

3 Submerge the piece of fabric in the dye in the plastic bowl. The areas held by the elastic bands will resist the dye and leave an interesting pattern when the bands are removed. Remove the fabric, squeeze out the excess dye, and let dry.

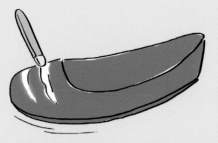

Be very careful with the bleach because it will remove color from most fabrics.

4 Meanwhile, ask an adult to carefully draw lines across the dyed shoes using household bleach and a popsicle stick. Watch as the bleach removes the dye and creates interesting zebra–like pattern on the shoes. Leave the shoes to dry again.

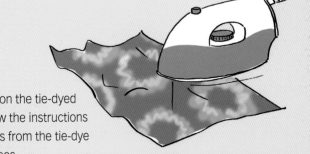

5 Remove the elastic bands on the tie-dyed fabric and iron it flat. Follow the instructions on page 11 to cut a pair of insoles from the tie-dye fabric and stick them into the shoes.

Chapter 5

Paper, paint, and plastic

Funky collage

Collage is such a simple yet effective way to transform a pair of shoes. You can make them really personal by carefully choosing images that you are interested in—you could design your shoes around your favorite pop star or song lyrics. You could even use words from your favorite book!

You will need

- Newsprint or sewing pattern paper
- Pointed-toe shoes with small heel
- PVA glue and brush
- Selection of papers and images
- Scissors
- Small sequins, such as nail art sequins
- Varnish
- 6 buttons
- Glue gun
- Fabric for insole (optional)
- Pencil (optional)

1 Apply a basic covering of newsprint or pattern paper to each shoe as a starting point for your collage, using PVA glue and a brush.

2 Cut out photos, images from magazines, scraps from gift wrap, or words from old books and collage these onto the shoes at random. With collage you just need to keep working onto the design until you feel the shoes look busy enough and the colors are balanced.

3 When the shoes are well
covered and you are happy
with the design, spread a thin layer
of glue over each shoe. Sprinkle some
small sequins over the shoe and then
let them dry. When the shoes are dry,
cover the design with a hard-wearing
varnish to protect it.

You may
need some adult
supervision
for step 4

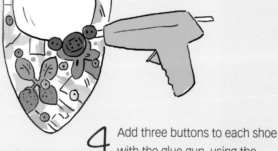

4 Add three buttons to each shoe
with the glue gun, using the
photograph as a guide for positioning.

5 To add a fabric insole to your shoes,
choose a suitable fabric to go with your
design and follow the instructions on page 11.

Gothic punk

Charms for your feet! These canvas boots have shoelace decorations and heat transfer motifs—create your own designs and you can guarantee nobody will have a pair the same.

You will need

- Templates on pages 125 and 126 or alternative images
- Shrink plastic sheet
- Pens and/or colored pencils
- Computer and printer
- Scissors
- Hole punch
- Baking pan
- Oven
- Oven mitts
- Pair of canvas baseball boots
- Needle and thread
- Templates on page 125 or alternative images
- Heat transfer sheet
- Iron

1 To make the shoelace charms, either use the templates on pages 126 or draw your own designs onto the sheet of shrink plastic. You could also print out images from your computer directly onto the rough side of the shrink plastic sheet.

The shrink plastic will shrink to about 40 per cent of the original height and width when baked, so take this into consideration when sizing images.

Make sure you print two of each image if you want the designs to be the same on each boot.

2 Cut out the images. Use a hole punch to make a hole in each side, or at each end, of the image. These will be used to stitch the charms onto the shoelace.

You may need some adult supervision for steps 3 and 6

3 Place the images on a Teflon baking pan or a baking pan lined with parchment sheet. Put them in a pre-heated oven at the temperature given in the manufacturer's instructions. The plastic will curl and move and then shrink and lay flat. Use oven mitts to take the baking pan out of the oven and let the charms cool down.

4 Arrange the charms onto the shoelaces as desired and use a needle and thread to stitch them on. Make sure that your laces are quite loose before stitching so that you can still get your foot inside the boots easily.

5 To make the design for the sides of the boot, either use the smaller skull and star templates on page 125, or find other images you like. Copy your chosen images onto a piece of heat transfer paper and then cut them out.

6 Position the images onto the boots wherever you would like them to go. Then following the manufacturer's instructions, transfer the images onto the canvas boot with an iron.

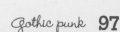

Galaxy sneakers

Galaxy design shoes are very fashionable at the moment and they are very easy to create. All you need are fabric paint and spray paint.

You will need

- Pair of canvas sneakers
- Paper towels or newsprint
- Masking tape
- Turquoise fabric paint
- Brush
- Blue and purple spray paint
- White fabric paint
- Fine paintbrush
- Fabric glitter glue

1 To prepare for painting the shoe, stuff it with paper towel or newsprint to prevent any of the spray paint getting inside and put masking tape around the edge of the sole to stop it being colored. Remove the shoelaces.

2 Paint each shoe with turquoise fabric paint using a wet brush. You may need to water the paint down a little bit depending on how thick it is. Try to cover each shoe evenly and then let them dry.

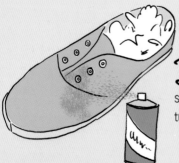

3 Use the blue and purple spray paint to spray small areas of the shoe—you should still be able to see some turquoise color coming through.

> You may need some adult supervision for step 3.

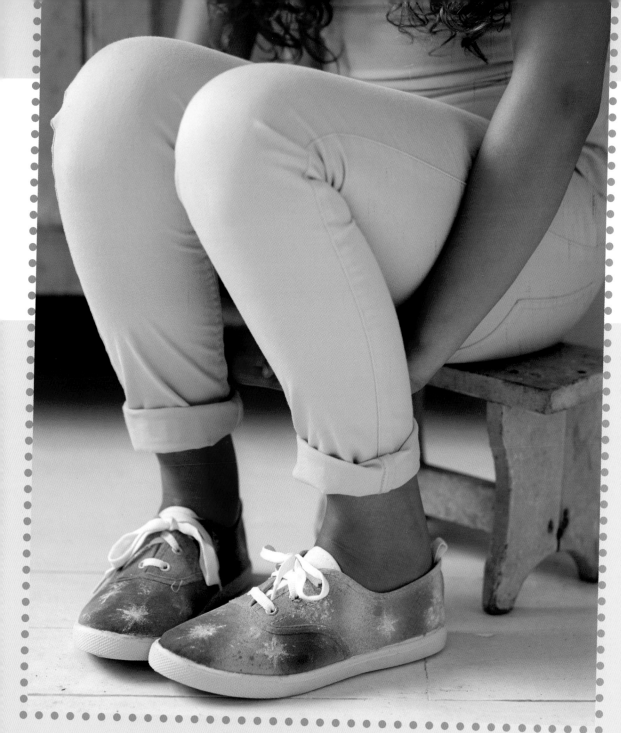

4 Use a little white fabric paint on a fine brush to create some stippled and dotted areas to look like planets and paint some little stars. Add some sparkle to the stars with the glitter glue.

5 Remove the tape and paper protecting each shoe and re-thread the laces—your galaxy sneakers are ready to wear!

Gatsby glitz

How cool are these painted fabric sneakers?
They are simple to make and look so effective—
all you need are a pair of plain fabric sneakers
or canvas deck shoes and some fabric paint.
They can easily be adapted with your favorite colors.

You will need

- Fabric sneakers
- Pencil
- Fabric paint
- Small brush
- Medium brush

1 Remove the shoelaces. With a pencil, draw faint lines to mark out the design using the photograph as a guide: an area at the toe of each shoe, around the laces, and down the back. Draw the edge of each area as a zigzag line.

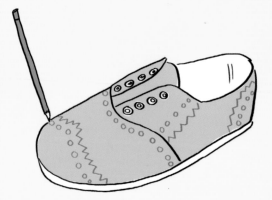

2 Draw small dots just inside each zigzag line and along the front seam line, following the photograph as a guide.

3 Paint to fill in the areas, leaving the dots in the painted areas unpainted. Paint in the dots along the seam line. Allow the paint to dry and put the laces back in.

Sunflower clips

Shrink plastic is a brilliant modern material that is a great way to make embellishments for shoes. You can create your own designs by drawing straight onto the plastic sheet or put it through your computer printer for more of a photographic style.

You will need

- Flower image
- Computer and printer
- 3–4 sheets of shrink plastic
- Scissors
- Baking pan
- Oven
- Oven mitts
- Curved bottle top
- Glue gun
- Small peg clip
- Pair of plain pumps
- Fabric for insole (optional)
- Pencil (optional)
- PVA or fabric glue (optional)

1 Scan a flower image that you like into your computer, or take a photo of a pretty flower using a digital camera and upload it onto the computer. Use one or two different flowers if you prefer. Cut and paste the image into a document.

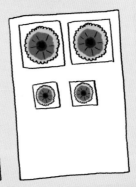

2 You will need six copies of the flower in total—you should be able to fit these onto two pages. Scale down the images so that you have three different sizes of flower (two large, two medium, two small). Remember that you need to create two sets of flowers (one of each size for each shoe). The shrink plastic will shrink to about 40 per cent of the original height and width when baked, so you should take this into consideration when you size your images. Print the flowers onto the shrink plastic sheets.

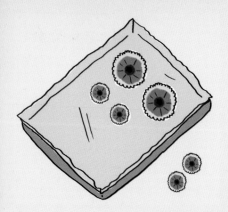

3 Cut out all of the flowers from the plastic sheet and place them on a Teflon baking pan or a baking pan lined with parchment sheet. Put them in a pre-heated oven at the temperature given in the manufacturer's instructions. The plastic will curl and move and then shrink.

You may need some adult supervision for steps 3, 4, and 5.

4 When the plastic shapes are flat again use oven mitts to take the baking pan out of the oven and quickly shape each flower over the top of a bottle to curve the edges up a little. The plastic is only pliable for a short time so you need to work quickly.

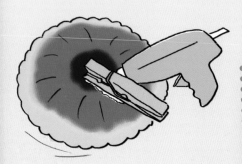

Don't bake the shrink plastic on a bare metal baking pan, waxed paper, or aluminum foil.

5 Place a small flower shape into the center of a medium one and use a glue gun to stick it in place. Then glue the medium flower into the center of a large flower. Repeat with the other set of flower shapes. To make the flowers detachable, glue a tiny peg onto the back, which can clip onto the front or strap of your pumps—you can then change the flowers from shoe to shoe.

6 To add a fabric insole to your shoes, choose a suitable fabric to go with your design and follow the instructions on page 11.

Cartoon style

If you enjoy drawing and painting then you will love this project. You could draw any of your favorite characters, shrink it down using the amazing shrink plastic, and sew it onto your cutest pair of heels.

You will need

- Template on page 123 or alternative image
- Shrink plastic sheet
- Pencil, paints, or watercolor pencils
- Hole punch
- Scissors
- Baking pan
- Oven
- Oven mitts
- 2 fabric circles each approx. 4 in. (10 cm) in diameter
- Needle and thread
- Fabric glue
- 6 in. (15 cm) of each of two coordinating trims
- Pair of heeled shoes
- Fabric for insole (optional)
- Pencil (optional)

1 Either use the Russian doll template on page 123 or choose your own favorite character, and draw or trace the image twice onto the shrink plastic sheet. Color in the drawings using watercolor paint or colored pencils (I used watercolor pencils).

The shrink plastic will shrink to about 40 per cent of the original height and width when baked, so take this into consideration when sizing images.

You may need some adult supervision for step 2.

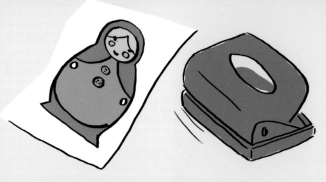

2 Punch a hole on either side of each character so you can sew it on. Cut around each character, place on a baking pan and put in the oven, following the shrink plastic instructions. Watch while the pieces curl up and shrink in size—when they are lying flat again remove the baking pan from the oven with oven mitts and let cool for a moment.

3 Make two yo-yos (Suffolk puffs) by turning under the edge of the fabric circle as you work a running stitch around it (see page 8). Pull the end of the thread (with the needle still attached) to gather the circle and tie both ends together to secure in place. Flatten the yo-yo down.

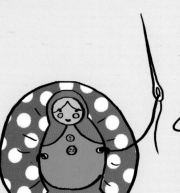

4 Sew the shrink plastic character onto the front of the yo-yo through the holes punched in step 2.

5 Use a little fabric glue to stick two lines of trim over the front of each shoe. Either glue a yo-yo in place on one side of each shoe or hand sew it on.

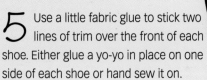

6 To add a fabric insole to your shoes, choose a suitable fabric to go with your design and follow the instructions on page 11.

Paisley sneakers

This is a really easy way of transforming a pair of low-cost fabric sneakers. All you need is a stencil and some fabric pens and you can add pattern in a color of your choice. The funky zipper laces add a unique finishing touch.

You will need

- Pair of white fabric sneakers
- Paisley template on page 122
- Blue, green, and red fabric paint pens
- Long metal zipper
- Scissors

1 Make the stencil (see page 15) from the template on page 122. Position the stencil over part of the shoe and color through the design with one of the fabric pens. Remove the stencil to reveal the design.

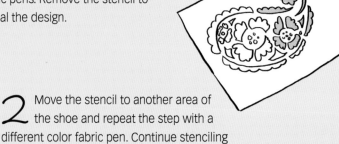

2 Move the stencil to another area of the shoe and repeat the step with a different color fabric pen. Continue stenciling until you are happy with the design.

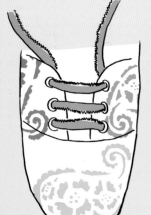

3 Remove the shoelaces. Open up the zipper fully and cut across it at the bottom above the zipper pull to split it into two pieces. Lace each piece through the holes in one shoe.

Don't forget to reverse the stencil on the other shoe for a matching design. Clean the paint off first though!

Spotty dotty

This is such a quick and easy design to create—to make your shoes stand out from the crowd all you need are a fine paintbrush and fluorescent fabric paint.

You will need

- Pair of canvas shoes
- Pencil
- Fine paintbrush
- Fluorescent fabric paint

1 Draw very faint pencil circles onto the trainers wherever you want to position a dot. Make some dots run off at the edges of the shoe so the design will look evenly spaced.

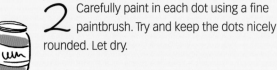

2 Carefully paint in each dot using a fine paintbrush. Try and keep the dots nicely rounded. Let dry.

Flower 'n' butterfly boots

Rain boots are such fun and come in so many different patterns but this project shows you how to add a bit of 3D bling—you will certainly stand out from the crowd.

You will need

- 48 in. (120 cm) of decorative trim
- Scissors
- Pair of rain boots
- Strong multi-purpose craft glue (optional)
- 8 in. (20 cm) square of red felt
- 4 x 8 in. (10 x 20 cm) of red dotted fabric
- 4 x 8 in. (10 x 20 cm) of white dotted fabric
- Flower and butterfly templates on page 124
- Pencil
- Small piece of aqua felt
- Small piece of dark blue felt
- Needle and thread
- 8 pearls

1 Cut the trim in half and tie in a bow (see page 10) around the top of the each boot. The boots I used had flaps with holes at the back to thread the ribbon through—if you are using boots without threading holes you will need strong glue to stick the bow in place at the back.

2 Fold each piece of felt and dotted fabric in half. Draw around the large flower and butterfly templates onto the red felt and cut out through both layers. Use the same templates to cut two large flowers from the folded red dotted fabric and two large butterflies from the folded white dotted fabric. Draw around the small flower template onto the folded aqua felt and the small butterfly template onto the folded dark blue felt and cut out each shape.

You need two sets of motifs, a set for each boot, so it saves time to fold each fabric in half and cut two of each piece at the same time.

3 Position a red dotted flower on top of a red felt flower and then add the small aqua felt flower to the center. Work a small running stitch around the center and pull to gather slightly—this will give the flower some shape. Stitch onto the fabric trim on one side of the boot and stitch a pearl into the center. Repeat to make another flower to add to the other boot.

4 Position a white dotted butterfly on top of a red felt butterfly then add a small blue butterfly to the center. Hand stitch the layers together and stitch three pearls down the center of the butterfly. Stitch the butterfly onto the trim, next to the flower. Repeat to make another butterfly to add to the other boot.

Aztec zigzags

Aztec zigzag patterns are very fashionable and this simple project shows you how to create an eye-catching zigzag pattern for a pair of canvas sneakers using sticky plastic.

You will need

- Strip of green sticky-back plastic
- Strip of cream sticky-back plastic
- Pencil and ruler
- Scissors
- Pair of black canvas sneakers

1 On the paper backing of each strip of sticky-back plastic, mark out approximately 24 triangles, and cut them out. Remove the paper backing from the first green triangle.

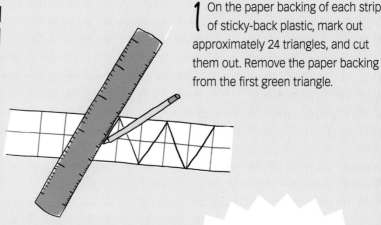

2 Stick the first triangle in the center and at the top of the front area of each sneaker, with the base aligned with the stitching and the point toward the toe. Add more green triangles in a row on either side to build up the design.

My sticky-back plastic had a grid on the paper backing that was great to get triangles the same size. If you are using plastic without a grid, make a template and draw all the triangles on the paper backing before cutting.

3 Now add a row of white triangles across the front pointing the other way, with the points between the green triangles to make the first zigzag. Add a second row of green triangles across the base of the white triangles to make diamonds.

4 Keep adding rows, creating zigzags and diamond shapes across the shoes, following the photograph as a guide. Along the sole, trim off any excess plastic so the design finishes neatly at the top of the sole.

Measure for measure

Create an unusual loopy flower using a simple tape measure and add a brightly colored button as the center.

You will need

- 2 self-cover buttons
- Scrap of fabric
- Scissors
- Needle and thread
- Fabric tape measure (much easier to stitch than a plastic one)
- Glue gun
- Shoes

You may need some adult supervision for step 4.

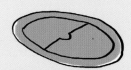

1 Cut a circle of fabric approx. ⅝ in. (1.5 cm) larger than the diameter of the button and work running stitch around the edge, leaving the needle still attached at the end. Gather the circle slightly and insert the front of the self-cover button, then gather the fabric fully and tie off. Push the back of the button on until you hear it "click" into place. Repeat for the other button.

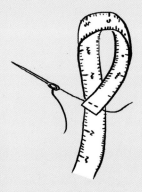

2 Cut the tape measure in half. Pick up one length and take hold of one end. Bring the rest of the tape round and back so that it sits under the end and makes the first loop petal. Secure in place with a couple of stitches.

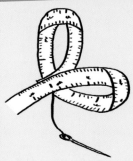

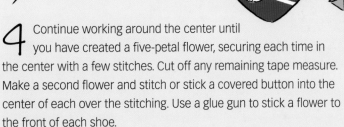

3 Bring the long end of the tape measure around again next to the first loop to make the second loop petal. Secure in the center with a couple of stitches.

4 Continue working around the center until you have created a five-petal flower, securing each time in the center with a few stitches. Cut off any remaining tape measure. Make a second flower and stitch or stick a covered button into the center of each over the stitching. Use a glue gun to stick a flower to the front of each shoe.

Chapter 6

Templates

Templates

This section contains all the templates you will need to make the projects in this book. Always read the labels carefully to check the size of the template you're using. Most of them are full-size templates and can be traced off the page; some are half-size templates, which means that you'll need to photocopy them at 200% to double the size of them.

Dinosaur slippers
page 56

Spikes (including seam allowance)

Pussy-cat bows
page 60

Eye

Inner ear

Outer ear

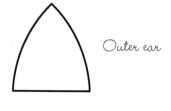
Nose

Little white mice
page 63

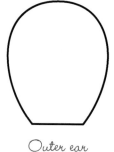
Outer ear

Inner ear

Nose

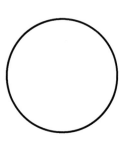
Outer eye

Inner eye

Dinosaur slippers and Monster slippers
pages 55 and 66

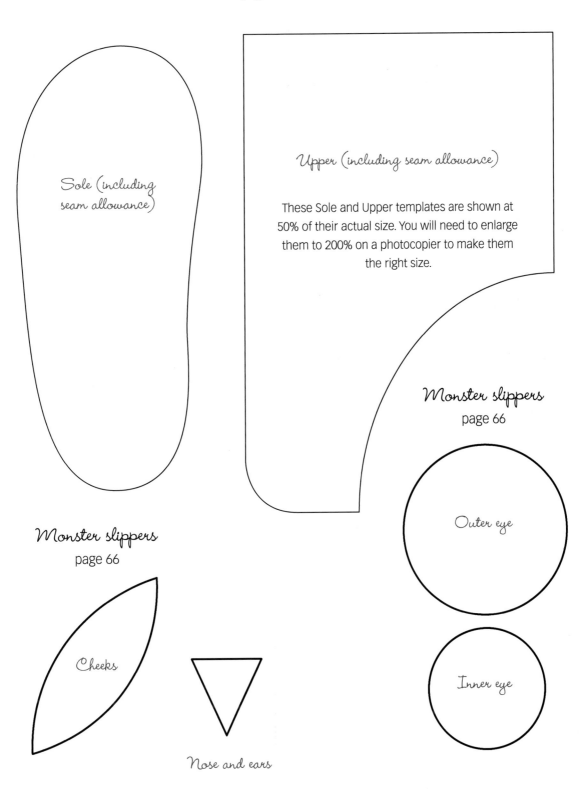

Sole (including seam allowance)

Upper (including seam allowance)

These Sole and Upper templates are shown at 50% of their actual size. You will need to enlarge them to 200% on a photocopier to make them the right size.

Monster slippers
page 66

Outer eye

Inner eye

Monster slippers
page 66

Cheeks

Nose and ears

Paisley sneakers
page 108

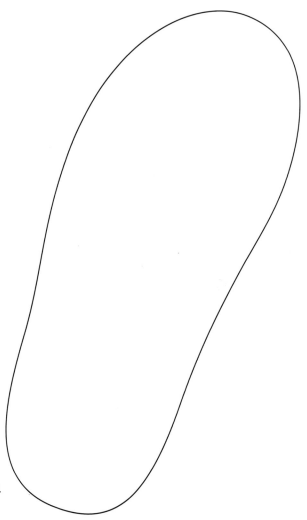

Flower sandals
page 22

Big bows
page 81

This template is shown at 50% of its actual size.
You will need to enlarge it to 200% on a
photocopier to make it the right size.

Matryoshka pumps
page 28

Face

Head scarf

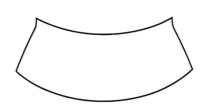

Collar

Cartoon style
page 105

Flower 'n' butterfly boots
page 112

Gothic punk
page 95

The larger skull and the largest star are for the shrink-plastic lace decorations. The smaller stars and skull are for the stick-on decorations.

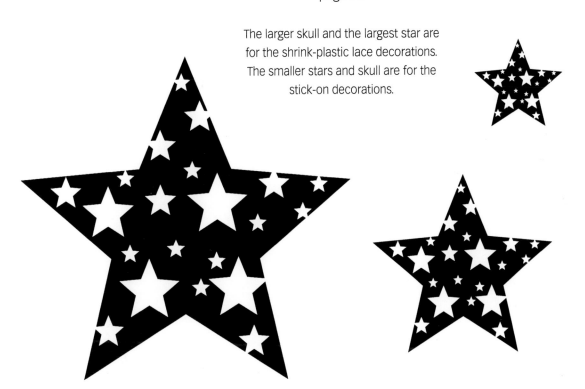

Gothic punk continued

page 95

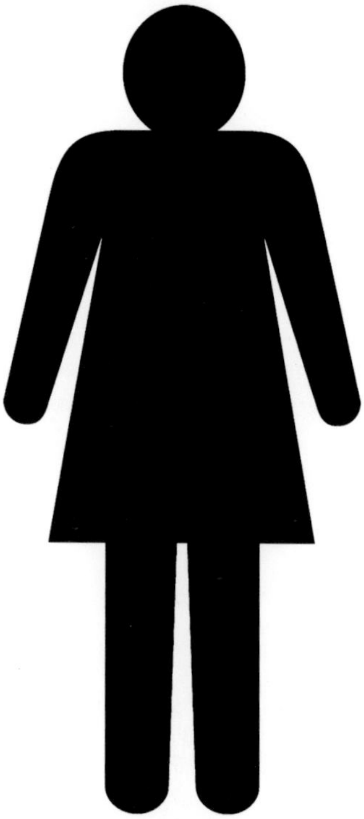

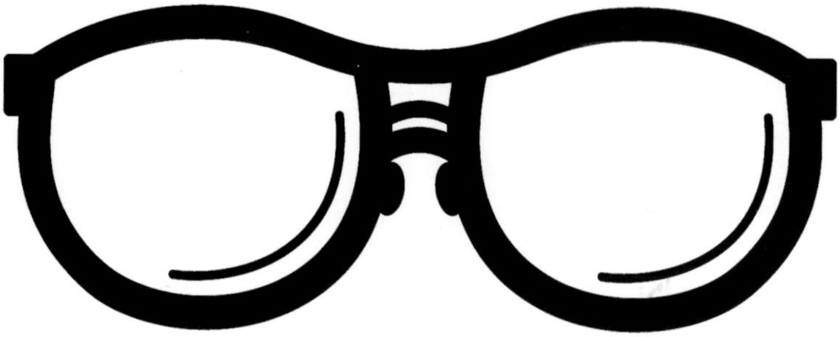

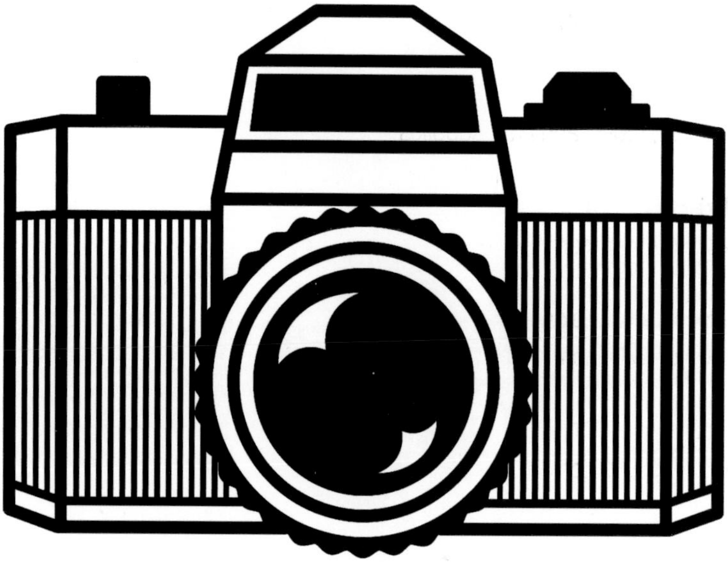

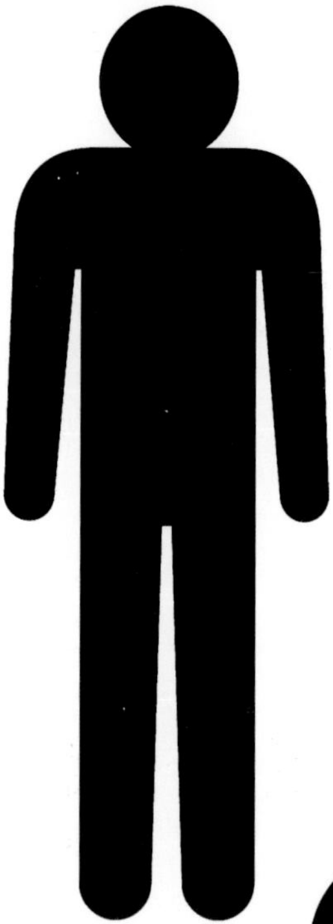

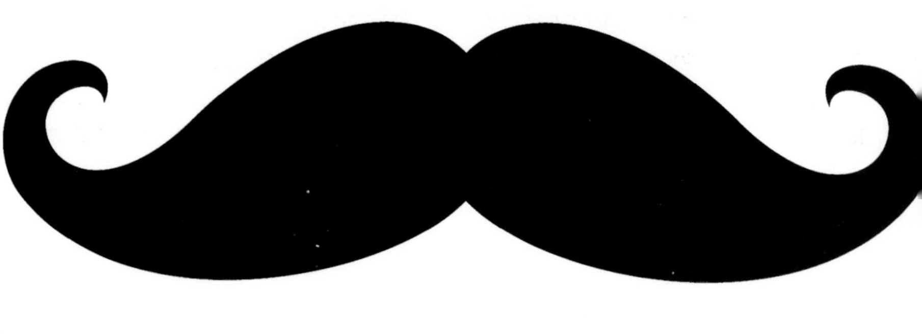

Suppliers

A.C. Moore (US)
www.acmoore.com

Baker Ross (UK)
www.bakerross.co.uk

Coats Crafts (UK)
www.coatscrafts.co.uk

Create for Less (US)
www.createforless.com

eBay (worldwide)
www.ebay.com
www.ebay.co.uk
For shoes, fabric, and craft supplies

Fabricland (US)
www.fabricland.com

Fabricville (Canada)
www.fabricville.com

Hobby Craft (UK)
www.hobbycraft.co.uk

Hobby Lobby (US)
www.hobbylobby.com

Homecrafts Direct (UK)
www.homecrafts.co.uk

John Lewis (UK)
www.johnlewis.com

Michaels (US/Canada)
www.michaels.com

Rowan Yarns (Worldwide)
www.knitrowan.com

Schachenmayr (US/Canada)
us.schachenmayr.com
For SMC yarn.

Wizard Limited (UK/US)
www.wizardtoys.com
For Shrinkles shrink-art plastic supplies.

Acknowledgments

I would like to thank Penny Craig, Marie Clayton, and everyone at CICO who has worked with me on this book—It has been a fantastic opportunity to indulge my passion for decorating and embellishing shoes! Thank you to my lovely husband Danny for his "up front" feedback on my shoe projects, and his endless computer help (he keeps reminding me that he does in fact have his own job and that he isn't my "IT Techy")—anyway I certainly appreciate his continuous help and support. I would finally like to thank my parents and in-laws, who have helped enormously with child care so that I could free up some time to get the book finished—you have been invaluable!

Index